AR Quiz No. 100876   BL 3.6   Pts. .5

I Like Biographies!

Read About
Tiger Woods

Stephen Feinstein

Enslow Elementary

an imprint of

Enslow Publishers, Inc.

40 Industrial Road   PO Box 38
Box 398   Aldershot
Berkeley Heights, NJ 07922 Hants GU12 6BP
USA   UK

http://www.enslow.com

Words to Know

amateur—One who does not play for money.

champion—A winner.

golf course—An area of land for playing golf.

Masters Tournament—One of the most important golf tournaments in the United States.

pro—Professional, or one who plays for money.

stroke—A swing to hit a ball.

tournament—A series of games.

Enslow Elementary, an imprint of Enslow Publishers, Inc.

Enslow Elementary® is a registered trademark of Enslow Publishers, Inc.

Copyright © 2005 by Enslow Publishers, Inc.

All rights reserved.

No part of this book may be reproduced by any means without the written permission of the publisher.

Library of Congress Cataloging-in-Publication Data

Feinstein, Stephen.
    Read about Tiger Woods / Stephen Feinstein.
      p. cm. — (I like biographies!)
    Includes bibliographical references and index.
    ISBN 0-7660-2594-2
    1. Woods, Tiger—Juvenile literature. 2. Golfers—United States—Biography—Juvenile literature. I. Title. II. Series.
    GV964.W66F47 2005
    796.352'092—dc22
        [B]
                        2004018942

Printed in the United States of America

10 9 8 7 6 5 4 3 2 1

To Our Readers: We have done our best to make sure all Internet Addresses in this book were active and appropriate when we went to press. However, the author and the publisher have no control over and assume no liability for the material available on those Internet sites or on links to other Web sites. Any comments or suggestions can be sent by e-mail to comments@enslow.com or to the address on the back cover.

Every effort has been made to locate all copyright holders of material used in this book. If any errors or omissions have occurred, corrections will be made in future editions of this book.

Illustration Credits: AP/Wide World, pp. 3, 5, 13, 15, 19, 21; Corbis, p. 7; Rudy Duran, pp. 1, 11; Optimist International, p. 17; Photos.com, p. 9.

Cover Illustration: AP/Wide World.

Contents

Eldrick "Tiger" Woods was born in California on December 30, 1975. His father, Earl, gave him the nickname Tiger.

Earl enjoyed playing golf. He practiced hitting golf balls into a net in his garage. When Tiger was six months old, Earl began bringing him into the garage. Tiger would sit in a highchair, watching Earl's every move.

Tiger Woods is one of the greatest golfers ever. He likes to help kids learn to play golf, too.

One day, when Tiger was eleven months old, he climbed out of the highchair. Tiger picked up his toy golf club. He swung at a golf ball and hit it into the net! When Tiger's mother Kultida came to the garage, Tiger did it again. It was a magic moment. Earl and Kultida knew that Tiger had been born to play golf.

Tiger had fun hitting golf balls, just like this girl.

Golf is all about hitting a ball into a hole with the fewest strokes possible. It looks easy, but it is really very hard. To become good at golf takes a lot of practice. Earl saw how much Tiger loved hitting golf balls. So even though Tiger was a baby, Earl let him practice as much as he wanted.

It is very hard to get the ball into the hole. Sometimes it stops right on the edge!

In 1978, when Tiger was two, Earl took him to a golf course. Tiger swung at the ball with his small club. The hole was 410 yards away. But Tiger got the ball in the hole with just eleven strokes.

Later that year, a TV reporter did a show about Tiger. Then, in October, Tiger went on the *Mike Douglas Show*, another TV show.

Tiger was famous before he was three years old. In this picture he is with Rudy Duran, a coach who helped him learn to play golf.

Chapter 3
Tiger Keeps His Eye on the Ball

In the next few years, Earl spent a lot of time teaching Tiger. He taught Tiger the different ways of hitting the ball. He taught him how to pick the right golf club for each type of stroke. He also taught Tiger how to keep his *eye* on the ball no matter what.

Earl helped Tiger become a champion. Sometimes Earl would make a noise when Tiger was about to hit the ball. This helped Tiger learn not to be bothered by noise when he played.

Before Tiger began playing golf, most golfers were white men. Tiger is a person of color—part black, part white, part American Indian, and part Asian. When Tiger began playing in golf tournaments, some people called him ugly names. But Tiger just kept his eye on the ball and he won almost every game.

Kultida, Tiger's mom, is very proud of him. She taught him not to get mad about mean things that people said.

As Tiger grew older, he became more and more famous. Fans loved to watch him hit the golf ball. His swing was perfect. Often he would hit the ball a very long way. It just kept going and going.

Tiger played in tournaments with much older golfers and often won.

In 1984, when he was eight, Tiger won his first junior golf championship. As a teenager, he won the title of U. S. Amateur Champion three years in a row—something no one had ever done before. Tiger then turned pro. At twenty-one, he became the youngest player and the first person of color to win the Masters Tournament.

Tiger was very happy when he won the Masters Tournament.

At age twenty-five, Tiger had won all of the four major tournaments. Fans called this the "Tiger Slam."

Thanks to Tiger Woods, golf will never be the same again. Thousands of young fans all over the world look up to him.

21

1975—Tiger Woods is born on December 30 in Cypress, California.

1976—Tiger hits a golf ball for the first time.

1978—Tiger plays on a golf course; he appears on TV on the *Mike Douglas Show* on October 6.

1984—Tiger wins his first junior championship.

1991—Tiger becomes the youngest U.S. Junior Amateur Champion ever.

1996—Tiger turns pro.

1997—Tiger wins his first major championship, the Masters Tournament.

2000–2001—Tiger wins four major golf tournaments—the "Tiger Slam."

Learn More

Books

Collins, David R. *Tiger Woods: Golf Superstar.* Gretna, La.: Pelican Publishing, 1999.

Jensen, Julie. *Beginning Golf.* Minneapolis, Minn.: Lerner, 1995.

Kramer, S. A. *Tiger Woods: Golf's Young Master.* New York: Random House, 1998.

Walker, Pamela. *Tiger Woods.* New York: Children's Press, 2001.

Internet Addresses

Official Junior Golf Web site
<www.juniorlinks.com>

Role Models on the Web
<http://www.rolemodel.net/tiger/tiger.htm>

Time for Kids Meets Tiger Woods
<http://www.timeforkids.com/TFK/kidscoops/story/0,14989,396393,00.html>

Index